P9-BJE-977

Living the New Life

*A practical guide in becoming born again
and filled with the Holy Spirit.*

By Casey Treat

Copyright © 1990
Casey Treat
All Rights Reserved
Printed in U.S.A.

**Scripture quotations (unless otherwise
indicated) are taken from The Holy Bible,
New International Version,
used by permission of New York
International Bible Society © 1978, by
New York International Bible Society.
Scripture Quotations marked KJV
are taken from the
King James Version of the Bible
and are used by permission.**

Fifth Printing, 1991

ISBN 0-931697-17-4

Table of Contents

Becoming Born Again

Receiving the Baptism
of the Holy Spirit

Table of Contents (Cont.)

Preface

Being born of the Spirit and filled with the Spirit are the greatest events of your life. These experiences change your eternal destiny as well as your daily life.

I am praying that this book will start you on a journey with God that will bring the greatest fullfillment to your life that is possible both now and forever.

Casey Treat

Becoming Born Again

I'll never forget the first day I walked into an alive church service. Everything about it was new and strange to me. Not only did I not know many people but I did not understand most of what they said. The Christian church has many words that are uncommon to most people. This little book is to assist you in understanding what the words "born again" mean and how to **Live the New Life**. In the next few pages you'll learn why every person must be born again, how to be born again and what it means to be born again. You'll also gain some insight on what to do now that you are born again so you can live a happy, successful Christian life.

The scripture verses in this book are from the New International Version Bible. Other translations that are good to study are the

King James Version, the Amplified Bible and the New American Standard Bible. If you do not know where the different books of the Bible are, look in the front of your Bible and you will find a list of the books contained in the Bible. Go to the page listed there and you will see chapter and verse numbers. A reference such as John 3:3 means you will find that verse in the book of John, chapter three and verse three.

1. Why must every person be born again?

Jesus was the first person to use the words "born again." He was speaking to a very high religious official named Nicodemus and He said,

> *"Unless a man is born again, he cannot see the kingdom of God."*   *(John 3:3)*

Nicodemus thought Jesus was talking about a second physical birth so he did not understand. Many people today think as Nicodemus did and are trying to figure out exactly what this new birth is all about.

Jesus then went on to explain,

> *"Flesh gives birth to flesh, but the Spirit gives birth to spirit."*   *(John 3:6)*

This means that physically speaking we were already born, but spiritually speaking we still need to be born. Our physical body is born but our human spirit is not. When

Adam rejected the Lord and obeyed the devil (Genesis 3) he died spiritually. God told Adam,

> *"But you must not eat from the tree of the knowledge of good and evil, for when you eat of it you will surely die."*
> *(Genesis 2:17)*

We know that Adam did not physically die on that day, for he lived to be 930 years old. What died that day was Adam's spirit man. That is, the real person that lives on the inside of the body. Your body is a house in which the real you, a spirit man, lives.

When Adam's spirit died, he was spiritually separated from the Father God. From that point on, all of his children were born spiritually dead and separated from God. Natural men have no fellowship or right standing with the Father. This is apparent by looking at all the ungodly things happening in the world today.

When Jesus told Nicodemus,

> *"You must be born again,"(John 3:7)*

he was saying that every man is already physically born, but he must be spiritually born in order to go to heaven. Without being born again you have no fellowship with the Lord, therefore you have no relationship. You can go to church, read the Bible and be a good person, but unless your spirit gets born again you cannot go to heaven or have fellowship with the Lord.

Jesus did not suggest that people be born again, He said,

"You must be born again." (John 3:7)

That is a commandment that cannot be avoided if you want a relationship with the Lord Jesus and the Father.

Those who refuse to be born again will never have eternal life and will never have a relationship with the Father God. When they die physically, they will be separated from God for eternity and exist in the torment of hell forever.

Those who are born again have eternal life in them. Jesus said,

"I tell you the truth, whoever hears my word and believes him who sent me has eternal life and will not be condemned; he has crossed over from death to life."
(John 5:24)

They will never die spiritually. When their physical body stops functioning they will go to meet the Lord in heaven and live with him throughout eternity.

2. How to Become Born Again

The Bible is the foundation for everything the Christian believes. What we feel or think is not always the truth, but the Word of God is. Therefore, we must look to the Word to find out how to become born again. I John 5:1 says,

> *"Everyone who believes that Jesus is the Christ is born of God."*

This is the basic principle of how to become born again. There are several points within this simple statement that you must understand.

1. It's for everyone.

Notice that salvation or the new birth is not limited to a certain group of people. It matters not what age, color, culture, or social class that you come from, there is not one person that cannot become born again. The apostle Peter said,

"And everyone who calls on the name of the Lord will be saved." *(Acts 2:21)*

You are an everyone, so you are included in those that can become born again.

2. You must believe.

This does not mean just to think about something. To believe in Jesus means to have faith, confidence and trust in Him. The Bible teaches that faith has corresponding actions.

"In the same way, faith by itself, if it is not accompanied by action, is dead."
(James 2:17)

Some people feel as long as they say they believe in Jesus they will go to heaven no matter how they live. They have the attitude that it is okay for a Christian to drink, smoke, lie, be lazy and have negative behavior. They think that just as long as they believe, they will go to heaven. You can see that is wrong. *When you believe in Jesus, then you will act the way He did.*

You will live the kind of life that Jesus lived on earth. Of course, none of us are perfect, and there will always be things that we are changing in order to grow. It is important to realize that believing also has action.

3. You must say it.

When you believe in Jesus as your Lord and Savior, it will come out of your mouth. Paul said we must "Confess with our mouth 'Jesus is Lord.'" In Matthew 10:32, 33 Jesus said,

> *"Whosoever therefore shall confess me before men, him will I confess also before my Father which is in heaven. But whosoever shall deny me before men, him will I also deny before my Father which is in heaven."*
>
> *King James Version (KJV)*

Part of being born again is confessing before others that Jesus is our Lord and we will follow Him.

4. Jesus is Lord.

This means that Jesus is the Messiah, Savior or Lord. There is no other person or god that holds this position. Only Jesus is Savior, only He is Lord over all the earth. Talking about Jesus in Acts 4:12, Peter said,

"Salvation is found in no one else, for there is no other name under heaven given to men by which we must be saved."

Jesus is not "a" way to heaven or "one" way to heaven, **He is the only way.** He said in John 14:6,

"I am the way and the truth and the life. No one comes to the Father except through me."

When you believe in Jesus as the Christ, you make Him the Lord of your life. That means He is the supreme authority, master or boss of your life. If Jesus is not your Lord, you are not born again. Paul said in Romans 10:9,

"That if you confess with your mouth,

'Jesus is Lord,' and believe in your heart that God raised him from the dead, you will be saved."

When you say "Jesus is Lord," that is a confession of submission. You are turning your life over to Jesus and now He is your supreme authority. A Christian does not do his own thing and live like the world. The Bible says we are not to order our lives like other people who are not born again. When Jesus is Lord, we follow His standards for life and obey His teachings in the Bible. Sometimes you may not feel like doing the Word and it may not be the easiest way, but it is the Christian way. When Jesus is Lord, He is Master and Leader of all we do.

When you believe in your heart and confess "Jesus is Lord," God does something inside of you. The real you, the spirit man, is recreated and becomes alive. Remember, Jesus said,

"...the Spirit gives birth to spirit."

(John 3:6)

The Holy Spirit comes into your life and causes your human spirit to be born again. This is not something that you can figure out with your mind — it is just a spiritual fact. II Corinthians 5:17 tells us,

"Therefore, if anyone is in Christ, he is a new creation; the old has gone, the new has come!"

When you believe in Jesus and confess Him as Lord you are changed inside. Not your body and not your mind, but the real you, the spirit man. You probably won't feel any different and you won't look any different but spiritually speaking, you are a new creature! You are no longer separated from God. You now are born of the Holy Spirit. You have fellowship with the Father and Jesus. Your name is written in The Book of Life and you are a part of the family of God.

Let's pray this simple prayer. Say it out loud sincerely.

"God, I believe Jesus is raised from the dead, and is alive right now. I confess Jesus is my Lord, and Master of my life. Thank you, I am saved. Amen."

3. Being Baptized in Water

One of the first steps to take after you are born again is to be baptized. You may think, "Why do I have to be baptized?" or "Well, my parents baptized me when I was a baby." Let's take a look at what the Bible has to say about baptism.

1. Water baptism is to take place after you are born again.

In Acts chapter 8, Philip, an evangelist, told an Ethiopian eunuch the good news about Jesus.

"As they [Philip and the eunuch] traveled along the road, they came to some water and the eunuch said, 'Look, here is water. Why shouldn't I be baptized?'

"Philip said, 'If you believe with all your heart, you may.' The official answered,

'I believe that Jesus Christ is the Son of God.'"   *(Acts 8:36, 37)*

Notice Philip said,

"If you believe with all your heart, you may."

We believe *first* and then are baptized.

Infants and small children are not yet able to confess Jesus as their Lord and Savior and should not be baptized. We are to pray over our infants and dedicate them to the Lord. Jesus said,

"Let the little children come to me, and do not hinder them, for the kingdom of God belongs to such as these. I tell you the truth, anyone who will not receive the kingdom of God like a little child will never enter it."

(Mark 10:14,15)

After our children are old enough to become born again, they are able to be baptized.

It is God's will that believers are baptized in water after they are born again.

> *"He [Jesus] said to them, 'Go into all the world and preach the good news to all creation. Whoever believes and is baptized will be saved, but whoever does not believe will be condemned.'"*
>
> *(Mark 16:15,16)*

2. Although you are commanded to be baptized, baptism alone will not save you.

When Jesus was being crucified, one of the criminals hanging on the cross next to Him said:

> *"'Lord, remember me when thou comest into Your kingdom.'*
>
> *"And Jesus said to him, 'Verily I say unto thee, today shalt thou be with Me in Paradise.'"*   *(Luke 23:42,43 KJV)*

The criminal did not have the opportunity to come down off of the cross and be baptized. However, he confessed Jesus as Lord. And Jesus told him,

> *"Today you will be with Me in Paradise."*

This does not mean that we are only baptized

if we want to be. Jesus commanded,

> *"Therefore go and make disciples of all nations, baptizing them in the name of the Father and of the Son and of the Holy Spirit."* (Matthew 28:19)

3. Baptism is an outward expression of our salvation and our obedience to the Lord Jesus Christ.

When we are baptized, we are immersed or totally submerged in water. The story in Acts tells us that when Philip baptized the eunuch,

> *"Then both Philip and the eunuch went down into the water and Philip baptized him."* (Acts 8:38)

Notice that they went *down into* the water, and in verse 39 it says they *came up out of* the water. It is important that we stay scriptural instead of following religious traditions.

4. Water baptism is an outward sign of what has happened inwardly after we are born again.

> *"Don't you know that all of us who were*

17

> *baptized into Christ Jesus were baptized into his death? We were therefore buried with him through baptism into death in order that, just as Christ was raised from the dead through the glory of the Father, we too may live a new life."*
>
> *(Romans 6:3-5)*

Our submersion is a symbol of the death of our old self, and our coming out of the water is a symbol of the new life Jesus has given us.

Receiving the Baptism
of the Holy Spirit

This section was written to help God's people receive the fullness of life in the Spirit. Many born again people think they have received all that God has, but they are not entering into the fullness of the Holy Spirit. It is one thing to be "born" of the Spirit, but it is another thing to be "filled" with the Spirit.

The baptism with the Holy Spirit is a necessary part of the successful Christian life. Jesus did not suggest to His disciples that they be baptized with the Holy Spirit, He commanded them to wait in Jerusalem and go nowhere until they had been endued (filled) with power from on high. If we are disciples of Jesus, that commandment is still for us today. Jesus wants you to be filled with the Holy Spirit and receive the power therein to live victoriously in every aspect of life.

In the pages to come, you will learn what the baptism with the Holy Spirit is, how to receive it, and how it will benefit your life according to the Word of God. Throughout this section, I will use the terms baptized with the Holy Spirit, baptized with the Holy Ghost and filled with the Spirit interchangeably, as the Bible does; they are synonymous phrases (they all mean the same thing).

4. What is the Baptism with the Holy Spirit?

The baptism with the Holy Spirit is a filling of the whole life of a believer with the supernatural power of the Spirit. We are **born** of the Spirit to be a part of God's family. We are **filled** with the Spirit to be victorious and fruitful in God's family.

In the last hours of Jesus' ministry on earth He left explicit directions with His followers,

> *"I am going to send you what my Father has promised; but stay in the city until you have been clothed with power from on high."*   *(Luke 24:49)*

> *"He [Jesus] gave them this command: 'Do not leave Jerusalem, but wait for the gift my Father promised, which you have heard me speak about. For John baptized with water, but in a few days you will be*

*baptized with the Holy Spirit...You will
receive power when the Holy Spirit comes
on you; and you will be my witnesses in
Jerusalem, and in all Judea and Samaria,
and to the ends of the earth."*

(Acts 1:4,5,8)

He commanded them to wait until they
were filled with the Holy Ghost. If it was that
important to Jesus, it should be that important to us. The 120 men and women that
believed in Jesus did just what He said. They
stayed together in an upper room and prayed
in one accord, waiting for what Jesus had
told them would happen. The Bible tells us
what happened after they had waited for 10
days:

*"When the day of Pentecost came, they
were all together in one place. Suddenly
a sound like the blowing of a violent wind
came from heaven and filled the whole
house where they were sitting. They saw
what seemed to be tongues of fire that*

separated and came to rest on each of them. All of them were filled with the Holy Spirit and began to speak in other tongues as the Spirit enabled them."

(Acts 2:1-4)

The day of Pentecost was a Jewish feast day that came 50 days after the Passover feast which is when Jesus was crucified. God chose this day to release the fullness of the Holy Spirit in the lives of those believers. Notice that they were **all** filled with the Holy Spirit; men, women, young or old, they **all** received. This was the beginning of the New Testament church age, which we are now in. We are a part of the same church these 120 people were. We have the same Father, same Savior, same Spirit, same Word, and same faith. They were the beginning of what is still happening today. The experiencing of the new birth and the baptism of the Holy Spirit will go on just like Acts chapter two, until Jesus returns.

Not the New Birth

Let's talk about what the Holy Spirit is not. To be filled or baptized with the Holy Spirit is not the same thing as being born of the Spirit. It is one thing to be born, it is another thing to be filled. Jesus said,

"I tell you the truth, unless a man is born again, he cannot see the kingdom of God."   *(John 3:3)*

Then He explained it further in John 3:6,

"Flesh gives birth to flesh, but the Spirit gives birth to spirit."

When a natural person makes Jesus the Lord, or supreme authority of his life, by confessing with his mouth and believing in his heart according to Romans 10:9, then he is born again or born of the Spirit. This is what makes us Christians part of God's family. This new birth is an act of the Holy Spirit imparting life or God's nature to our human spirit. When the Holy Spirit, or the life of God, comes in contact with our dead human spirit, a change takes place. We are recreated spiritually. Paul said it like this,

"Therefore, if anyone is in Christ, he is a new creation; the old has gone, the new has come!" *(II Corinthians 5:17)*

This is being born again or born of the Spirit. Any man or woman in the world can be born again at any time. It is done by making Jesus your Lord and Master. Jesus said in John 14:16,17,

"And I will pray the Father and He shall give you another Comforter, that He may abide with you forever; even the Spirit of truth; whom the world cannot receive, because it seeth Him not, neither knoweth Him, but you know Him; for He dwelleth with you and shall be in you." *(KJV)*

Notice, while talking about the Holy Spirit in this verse, He said that the world **cannot receive Him.** This "other comforter" could not be the act of being born again, because we were all in the world before we were born again. To receive what Jesus is talking about here, you must first get out of the world and into God's kingdom. He is speaking of the baptism with the Holy Spirit. When a person is born again they are no longer a part of the world, they are now able to receive the Spirit of truth or the Holy Ghost.

This is not to say that born again people do not have the Holy Spirit at all. They are born of the Spirit, but they don't have the full release of the Spirit in their lives. This takes place when they are baptized with the Holy Ghost.

John the Baptist told the people about the ministry of Jesus in John 1:33,

"I would not have known him, except that the one who sent me to baptize with water told me, 'The man on whom you see the Spirit come down and remain is he who will baptize with the Holy Spirit.'"

Notice that Jesus is the Baptizer with the Holy Spirit. To be born again is something that the Holy Spirit does. To be baptized with the Holy Spirit is something that Jesus does.

Jesus is the Baptizer with the Holy Ghost.

Even after reading these verses, some still have the idea that when you are born again, that's all there is. Let's look at a story that took place in the early church recorded in Acts chapter 8. An evangelist, named Philip, had gone down to Samaria and preached Jesus to the people there. The Bible says he had good results (Acts 8:5-8). Many of the people were born again and baptized in water.

> *"But when they believed Philip as he preached the good news of the kingdom of God and the name of Jesus Christ, they were baptized, both men and women."*   *(Acts 8:12)*

While this revival was still going on in Samaria, word got back to Jerusalem about what was going on. So, Peter and John came down to help out with the ministry. I want you to notice why they came.

> *"When the apostles in Jerusalem heard that Samaria had accepted the word of*

God, they sent Peter and John to them.
When they arrived, they prayed for them
that they might receive the Holy Spirit."
(Acts 8:14,15)

Many of the people already believed in Jesus. They were born again and even baptized in water, but they didn't have all that God had for them. If they had received it all when they were born again, then Peter and John would not have come down to pray for them to receive the Holy Ghost. Acts 8:16 says,

"...the Holy Spirit had not yet come upon
any of them, they had simply been
baptized into the name of the Lord Jesus."

It is one thing to be born of the Spirit, it is completely different to be filled with the Spirit.

In traveling to Ephesus, Paul found several disciples. He began to have fellowship with them and right away, sensed that there was something missing in their Christian experience, so he asked them,

"Did you receive the Holy Spirit when you believed?" *(Acts 19:2)*

Paul knew that being born again was not all that God had for His people. He wanted these disciples to not only believe in the Lord Jesus, but also to be baptized with the Holy Ghost. If they were the same experience he would not have asked them if they had received the Holy Ghost yet. We have millions of Christians who believe in Jesus, but they have not received the baptism with the Holy Spirit. I pray that they might hear the truth and receive the fullness of what God has for them.

5. The First Evidence

There is an initial evidence that takes place in the life of the believer when he is filled with the Holy Spirit. It is not a physical feeling. Some have thought (or have been told) that when you are filled with the Spirit "you will feel power go through you," "lightening bolts will go through your body," "glory balls will burst on your head," "shivers will go up your spine," or "the power of God will knock you to the floor." You may have heard one or more of these and they are lies. **Nowhere in the Bible is a physical feeling associated with the baptism of the Holy Spirit.** You do not feel the Spirit physically. (This is not to say that you never will, but a physical feeling associated with the Holy Ghost is not a normal occurrence.)

Others have said that when you are filled with the Spirit you'll never sin again or have any problems in your life. This also is a lie. The baptism with the Spirit will not instantly transform you into an angel and remove every negative circumstance. There will be positive changes because God's power is released in you, but not one big metamorphosis.

The initial evidence of being baptized with the Holy Spirit is that you will begin to speak with other tongues. Notice what Acts 2:4 says,

> *"All of them were filled with the Holy Spirit and began to speak in other tongues as the Spirit enabled them."*

They didn't roll on the floor, bark like a dog, climb the walls, hang from the chandelier, or foam at the mouth. They began to speak something. It was the language of the Holy Spirit, which the Bible calls other tongues. They were all sitting in prayer (not rolling, not jumping, not kneeling — sitting), and when they were filled with the Spirit, they began to speak with other tongues. This is the initial or first sign of being baptized with the Holy Spirit. Let's look at other Bible passages that state this.

One day Peter went to the house of a Gentile, named Cornelius, who had been seeking God. An angel had told Cornelius to send for Peter, so when Peter came, he began to teach them all about Jesus. He told how Jesus was the anointed one, and how He had healed all that were oppressed of the devil. The Bible says,

> *"While Peter was still speaking these words, the Holy Spirit came on all who heard the message. The circumcised believers who had come with Peter were astonished that the gift of the Holy Spirit had been poured out even on the Gentiles. For they heard them speaking in tongues and praising God."* *(Acts 10:44-46)*

Notice that the Holy Ghost fell on them that heard the Word and all the Jews were astonished. How did they know the Holy Ghost had filled them? Did they see Him? Did they feel Him? No, verse 46 gives the answer.

"For (or because) they heard them speaking in tongues and praising God."

The first thing that happened to these people when they were baptized with the Holy Spirit is they began to speak with other tongues.

Again in Acts 19, Paul ministered to some people in Ephesus. They had been baptized by John in water for repentance, but they knew nothing of the Holy Spirit. Acts 19:5,6 tells us:

"On hearing this, they were baptized in the name of the Lord Jesus. When Paul placed his hands on them, the Holy Spirit came on them, and they spoke in tongues and prophesied."

This situation was no different than the others. The first thing that happened when they were filled with the Spirit was they spoke with tongues. This is the initial evidence. Jesus said,

"Every matter may be established by the

testimony of two or three witnesses."
(Matthew 18:16)

I have given three passages (witnesses), so if you are scriptural, you must believe that speaking with tongues is for all who are filled with the Holy Spirit.

Some have said, "Tongues are of the devil!" That's just a statement of Bible ignorance. People are afraid of what they don't understand, so they do anything, including lie, to avoid it. Paul said,

"I thank God that I speak in tongues more than all of you."
(I Corinthians 14:18)

It's obvious Paul didn't believe tongues were of the devil. Somebody said, "I'll never go around any tongue talkers." Well, they will have a hard time in heaven being around Paul, Barnabas, Peter, John, Philip, Matthew and Mary (Jesus' mother); *they all spoke with other tongues.*

6. Who is the Baptism of the Holy Spirit For?

There are those who believe in being filled with the Spirit, but they say it is not for everyone. Let's check the Bible and see what God says. I'm always more interested in what God's Word says than in what anybody else says. John the Baptist said,

> *"The next day John saw Jesus coming toward him and said, 'Look, the Lamb of God, who takes away the sin of the world!'*
>
> *"I would not have known him, except that the one who sent me to baptize with water told me, 'The man on whom you see the Spirit come down and remain is he who will baptize with the Holy Spirit.'"*
> *(John 1:29,33)*

He said Jesus would take away the sin of the world and baptize with the Holy Ghost. Who is He going to baptize with the Holy Ghost?

The same people He took the sin away from. He provided the baptism with the Holy Spirit for them, too. Whoever will accept the forgiveness of sin that Jesus provided can also have the baptism with the Holy Ghost that Jesus provided.

In Acts 2:38,39, the Bible says,

"Peter replied, 'Repent and be baptized, every one of you, in the name of Jesus Christ so that your sins may be forgiven. And you will receive the gift of the Holy Spirit. The promise is for you and your children and for all who are far off — for all whom the Lord our God will call.'"

He said, whoever would repent (be born again), and be baptized in water would receive the gift of the Holy Ghost. Then, to make it clear that this is for everyone, he broke it down in detail. The promise is for:
1. You (all that were present)
2. For your children (all those born or not yet born)

3. All that are far off (everyone on earth at that time)
4. For all whom the Lord our God will call (all that would be born again throughout time).

There is no one that is left out. The baptism with the Spirit is for all people. Jesus said in Mark 16:17,

> *"And these signs will accompany those who believe: In my name they will drive out demons; they will speak in new tongues."*

Whoever **believes** will speak with new tongues. The only people who do not speak with tongues are those who do not believe. God can't make you do anything. You receive His gifts by faith. If you don't believe, you don't receive. Someone said, "If God wants me to speak with tongues, He'll make me." Wrong! Jesus said, *"This sign will follow those who believe."* In His name they will speak with new tongues.

In I Corinthians 12:30, when Paul asks,

"Do all speak in tongues?"

He is speaking of the gift of diverse kinds of tongues that are to be interpreted in the church service. This is one of the nine gifts of the Spirit listed in that chapter for the body of Christ. He is not speaking of the personal gift of tongues for the believer. They are **two different things.** It is just like the gift of faith listed in I Corinthians 12. All believers do not have diverse kinds of tongues that will be spoken out and interpreted in the body, but all can have the ability to pray in tongues for personal edification.

7. The Benefits of Speaking with Tongues

There are several very powerful benefits given to the Christian when speaking or praying in tongues. Because of these benefits you should develop a daily habit of praying in other tongues. Make it a part of your lifestyle to pray in the Spirit.

Praying in the Spirit:

1. Builds up the inner man.

> *"He who speaks in a tongue edifies himself."* (I Corinthians 14:4)

The inner man is the spirit and soul. When you pray in tongues, you edify or strengthen this inner man. One Greek scholar said that the word edify means to charge, like you would a battery. When we take the time to pray in the Spirit, the inner man is charged up. You are ready to release power out of your innermost being (John 7:38,39).

2. Allows us to receive revelation knowledge.

"For anyone who speaks in a tongue does not speak to men but to God. Indeed, no one understands him; he utters mysteries with his spirit."

(I Corinthians 14:2)

The Father wants to share mysteries or divine secrets with us, but He cannot do it through our minds. We receive revealed knowledge, not through our human spirit, but the Holy Spirit. When we pray in tongues on a regular basis, we open ourselves to the Holy Spirit to receive revelation knowledge or things that cannot be known by the natural mind alone. Paul said,

"I thank God that I speak in tongues more than all of you."

(I Corinthians 14:18)

He definitely had more revelation knowledge than any other man.

3. Enables you to hear the voice of your spirit.

"For if I pray in a tongue, my spirit prays,

but my mind is unfruitful."

(I Corinthians 14:14)

Sometimes our greatest problem is our mind or the way we think. God does not lead men by their minds. He works through the human spirit (Proverbs 20:27). When we pray in tongues, our minds are not involved, so we can hear our spirit.

4. Allows the Spirit to pray for things you don't know about.

"In the same way, the Spirit helps us in our weakness. We do not know what we ought to pray, but the Spirit himself intercedes for us with groans that words cannot express."   *(Romans 8:26)*

One of our greatest infirmities or weaknesses is not knowing how to pray. This is an inability to produce results, but the Holy Spirit wants to help us. When we are filled with the Spirit, He can pray through us with sounds that cannot be spoken in articulate speech — other tongues — and we will be praying for things that our natural minds don't even know about. This is one of the greatest tools of the believer: intercessory prayer in the Spirit.

5. Allows us to pray the perfect will of God.

"And he who searches our hearts knows the mind of the Spirit, because the Spirit intercedes for the saints in accordance with God's will."

(Romans 8:27)

We all face situations when we don't know God's will, but the Holy Spirit always knows the will of God. When we pray for a specific thing in other tongues, we can be sure we are praying the perfect will of God. In tongues, there is no unbelief, no mistakes, and no failure.

6. Builds you up on your faith.

"But you, dear friends, build yourselves up in your most holy faith and pray in the Holy Spirit." *(Jude 20)*

This does not say tongues will give you faith, but praying in the Spirit will build you up on your faith. At times, you may sense that your faith is weak. If you will pray in the Spirit for a time, it will lift you up and you then can put your faith to work.

7. Brings rest and refreshing.

"Very well then, with foreign lips and strange tongues God will speak to this people, to whom he said, 'this is the resting place, let the weary rest'; and, 'This is the place of repose' — but they would not listen."

(Isaiah 28:11,12)

Have you ever awakened after eight hours of sleep and still felt tired? It wasn't physical fatigue, but fatigue in the inner man. Isaiah prophesied that praying in tongues will bring rest and refreshing to the inner man. Even after hours of work, if you'll spend time praying in tongues, you will begin to be refreshed.

8. Helps us keep our tongue in line with the Word.

"The tongue also is a fire, a world of evil among the parts of the body. It corrupts the whole person, sets the whole course of his life on fire, and is itself set on fire by hell.

"But no man can tame the tongue. It is a restless evil, full of deadly poison.

"With the tongue we praise our Lord and Father, and with it we curse men, who have been made in God's likeness. Out of the same mouth come praise and cursing. My brothers, this should not be."

(James 3:6,8-10)

You will have what you say, so it's important to say the right thing. Natural man cannot tame the tongue, but with the help of the Spirit of God we can. When we pray in the Spirit, we are taming the tongue and submitting it to the Lord.

9. Gives thanks and magnifies God.

"Else when thou shalt bless with the

spirit...for thou verily givest thanks well.”
(I Corinthians 14:16,17, KJV)

"For they heard them speaking in tongues
and praising God.” *(Acts 10:46)*

There is no greater avenue of worship than
in the Spirit. Paul said he sang in the Spirit.
Jesus said true worship was in the Spirit
(John 4:24). If you have ever seen a body of
Spirit-filled believers worshipping God, you
can quickly see a tremendous difference.

10. Is a sign to unbelievers.

"Tongues, then, are a sign, not for be-
lievers but for unbelievers; prophecy,
however, is for believers, not for unbe-
lievers.” *(I Corinthians 14:22)*

Many are worried about offending non-Chris-
tians in church, so they don't allow speaking
in tongues in the service. The Bible teaches
that this sign will help the unbelievers to
realize that God is present and His power is
real. We shouldn't quench the gifts of God,
but encourage their manifestation.

8. How to Receive the Baptism with the Holy Spirit

Many people have prayed or had others pray for them to be filled with the Spirit, but never received anything. This fact often causes confusion, condemnation, or wrong thinking. Some have thought, "I must not be good enough," or "God doesn't want me to have it." God **does** want you to have it and here are some simple steps to enable you to receive.

1. Know that you are born again.
Only the born again believer is a candidate for the baptism with the Holy Spirit. The world cannot receive this experience (Romans 10:9,10; John 14:17).

2. Ask Jesus to baptize or fill you with the Spirit.
He said in Luke 11:11-13,

> *"Which of you fathers, if your son asks for a fish, will give him a snake instead?*

Or if he asks for an egg, will give him a scorpion? If you then, though you are evil, know how to give good gifts to your children, how much more will your Father in heaven give the Holy Spirit to those who ask him!"

3. Believe that you receive no matter how you feel or think.

We receive from God **by faith, not feelings.** You don't have to feel anything to receive the Holy Ghost (Mark 11:24; Hebrews 11:6).

4. Don't try to understand it with your mind.

I Corinthians 14:2 says,

"For anyone who speaks in a tongue does not speak to men but to God. Indeed, no one understands him; he utters mysteries with his spirit."

Your mind will never understand tongues, it's not supposed to. This is a spiritual experience, not a mental one.

5. After you've asked Jesus to fill you with the Holy Spirit, begin to speak sounds that are not English out of your mouth.

Your head will resist this and say, "it's foolish," "you're making this up," and use other reasoning, but this is not a mental experience. From your spirit, there will come sounds that don't make sense. Open your mouth, use your voice, lips and tongue to speak them out. God does not speak with tongues, and He will not make you do it. Acts 2:4 says,

> *"All of them were filled with the Holy Spirit and began to speak in other tongues as the Spirit enabled them."*

They did the speaking, not the Holy Ghost.

6. Relax and let yourself flow in the Spirit and pray boldly in other tongues for several minutes.

Jesus said Satan will always try to steal what we receive from God (Mark 4:15). Don't let him steal from you. You may start thinking all kinds of funny thoughts, or have doubts, but reject that thinking and believe the Bible. Remember, Jesus said, if you ask, the Father will give you the Holy Ghost and,

> *"These signs will accompany those who believe: In my name they will drive out demons; they will speak in new tongues."*
> *(Mark 16:17)*

Praying in other tongues is a great blessing to the body of Christ. It is a gift that all believers should cultivate and use regularly. You'll find great spiritual enrichment and strength as you spend time daily praying in the Spirit. Remember these words of the Apostle Paul,

> *"Therefore, my brothers, be eager to prophesy, and do not forbid speaking in tongues."* *(I Corinthians 14:39)*

The Next Step

This is just the beginning of your new life. These next few chapters will show you the specific areas to help you grow in your Christian walk.

9. Growing Up Spiritually

Being born again and baptized with the Holy Spirit is only the beginning. The Lord has many wonderful things for you as you grow in knowledge of the truth. Many times Christians don't realize they must grow and change. To be born again is just that, you are born. Now, just like a baby, you must grow up. I Peter 2:2 says,

"Like newborn babies, crave pure spiritual milk, so that by it you may grow up in your salvation."

One Bible translation says,

"Desire the sincere milk of the Word that ye may grow thereby." **(KJV)**

By growing in knowledge of the Word of God you will receive the spiritual food you need to grow up into spiritual maturity. Many people are born again but never eat spiritual food so they do not grow. Just imagine what would happen to a small baby if it had no mother to feed it. It would be only a few days until the child would starve to death. So it is with the spiritual babe. You must be fed a steady diet of the Word of God in order to grow in the Lord. Jesus said in John 8:32,

"If you hold to my teaching (Word), you are really my disciples. Then you will know the truth, and the truth will set you free."

If there are areas in your life that make you feel like you are in bondage, the truth will set you free. Many things cannot be prayed away or pushed aside, but by learning the truth you can change things and be free. Jesus desires for you to be happy, healthy and free. If there are problems in your life, the truth will enable you to overcome them and live the abundant life (John 10:10).

We read in II Timothy 3:16 and 17,

"All Scripture is God-breathed and is useful for teaching, rebuking, correcting and training in righteousness, so that the man of God may be thoroughly equipped for every good work."

The scriptures or the Word of God has been inspired by the Father. That means He spoke through men to give us the Bible. His Word is profitable to us for teaching, correcting and training for a successful Christian life. The reason many people suffer through life with problems and misery is because they don't understand the principles of the Bible. Notice that the verse tells us that the Word will prepare or equip you for **every good work**. By growing in knowledge of the scriptures you will be preparing for every aspect of Christian living.

10. Bible Reading Plan

The Bible has so much information that many times we get lost trying to figure out where to start, so I'll give you a simple plan to start learning the Word.

First, read through the book of Galatians in two different translations (i.e., New International Version and King James version). Don't read so fast that it does not make any sense to you. There is no value in just reading a lot of scripture. The important thing is that you gain knowledge and understanding.

Second, read through the book of James in two different translations. This will cause you to gain insight concerning faith and Christian behavior.

As you read and think about these two books, the Lord will help you to understand how to deal with things you face daily. If you have questions or points of confusion, do not hesitate to talk to another Christian or your pastor. After you have read those books two times each, go back to the first book of the New Testament, Matthew, and start reading each book. Remember, do not try to get through as fast as possible. Take time to meditate, ponder or think on scriptures so you can understand them. Just saying, "I read the whole New Testament" will not impress God. It is growing in knowledge and understanding that will help you.

Another vitally important part of growing up spiritually is going to church. You must find a church that will teach the Bible simply, clearly and with authority. Jesus always spoke simply so people could understand. If someone is speaking "over your head" it will not help you grow. Paul said in Hebrews 10:25,

> *"Let us not give up meeting together, as some are in the habit of doing, but let us encourage one another — and all the*

more as you see the Day approaching."

Get involved with a fired-up church that you feel you can grow in. They should be helping people to be filled with the Holy Spirit and speak with new tongues, laying hands on the sick and ministering to the needs of people. Through regular Bible teaching you will be spiritually strengthened. It will not happen overnight, but if you are consistent, growth will come.

11. Renewing Your Mind

Many people do not realize that the Christian life is one of change. That means you must be willing to give up your way of thinking and accept God's way of thinking. Every time you think in a way that is contrary to the Word, make a decision to give up your thoughts and accept God's thoughts. Romans 12:2 says,

> *"Do not conform any longer to the pattern of this world, but be transformed by the renewing of your mind. Then you will be able to test and approve what God's will is — his good, pleasing and perfect will."*

Notice that your mind must be renewed to do the will of God. You will find many areas of your life such as relationships, money, health, faith, talking and responsibility that you will have to change. As you learn the

Word of God, these areas will become apparent to you and then you can change your thinking. Don't try to make excuses or prove yourself right, just be willing to change. In this way God will be able to bless your life and there will be a steady increase of spiritual growth. Here again it will not happen all at once. This is a never-ending process.

The mind that is not renewed to the Word of God will stop you from walking with the Lord. Notice in Romans 12:2 Paul said to approve or do the will of God, you must be transformed. The English word transformed comes from the Greek word "metamorphoo." It means to change into another form. Every person that is born again has thinking that must be changed. As this happens, the mind is renewed and the good, pleasing and perfect will of God will then be fulfilled.

Paul said again in II Corinthians 10:4,5,

"The weapons we fight with are not the weapons of the world. On the contrary, they have divine power to demolish

strongholds. We demolish arguments and
every pretension that sets itself up
against the knowledge of God, and we
take captive every thought to make it
obedient to Christ."

From this scripture we see that our enemy, Satan, attempts to build up strongholds in our lives. These strongholds are thoughts and ideas that are contrary to the truth and keep us from a happy Christian life. Paul tells us to pull down every imagination (reasoning), and get "every thought" in line with Jesus or the Word of God. It is possible for you to control your thoughts and keep your thinking on positive things.

The enemy will try to put thoughts of doubt, confusion or negativity in your mind, but as you continue to replace your old way of thinking with the truth, the joy and peace of the Lord will grow strong in you.

Romans 8:5-8 says,

"Those who live according to the sinful
nature have their minds set on what the

nature desires; but those who live in accordance with the Spirit have their minds set on what the Spirit desires. The mind of sinful man is death, but the mind controlled by the Spirit is life and peace, because the sinful mind is hostile to God. It does not submit to God's law, nor can it do so. Those controlled by the sinful nature cannot please God."

The mind can agree with the flesh or sinful nature, and you will do what it desires, or the mind can agree with your spirit and you will do what the Holy Spirit desires. Your life has three parts to it, the flesh, the soul (mind, emotions and will) and the spirit. The flesh contacts the natural world and is where the sinful desires of man exist. The spirit contacts God and becomes a new creation when you are born again. The mind can go whichever way you decide, or will, for it to go. The mind can follow the flesh and negativity which leads to death, or you can renew your mind and make it follow the spirit which is life and peace. You have the ability to control your thoughts and keep them on positive things. At first it may seem hard, but as you grow it will be easier and the benefits will be greater.

Now that you are born again, continue to grow up in the Lord by being baptized with water, filled with the Holy Spirit and continually renewing you mind.

This new life has many wonderful things in store for you.

Notes